ORTS ON THE EDGE!

EXTREME BMX

WIL MARA

Marshall Cavendish
Benchmark
New York

NOTE FROM THE PUBLISHER:
Some early BMX riders, as well as some professional riders, have chosen at times not to wear safety gear. Do not attempt BMX riding without proper gear and safety precautions.

Website: www.marshallcavendish.us

This publication represents the opinions and views of the author based on Wil Mara's personal experience, knowledge, and research. The information in this book serves as a general guide only. The author and publisher have used their best efforts in preparing this book and disclaim liability rising directly and indirectly from the use and application of this book.

Other Marshall Cavendish Offices:
Marshall Cavendish International (Asia) Private Limited, 1 New Industrial Road, Singapore 536196 • Marshall Cavendish International (Thailand) Co Ltd. 253 Asoke, 12th Flr, Sukhumvit 21 Road, Klongtoey Nua, Wattana, Bangkok 10110, Thailand • Marshall Cavendish (Malaysia) Sdn Bhd, Times Subang, Lot 46, Subang Hi-Tech Industrial Park, Batu Tiga, 40000 Shah Alam, Selangor Darul Ehsan, Malaysia

Marshall Cavendish is a trademark of Times Publishing Limited

All websites were available and accurate when this book was sent to press.

LIBRARY OF CONGRESS CATALOGING-IN-PUBLICATION DATA
Mara, Wil.
Extreme BMX / Wil Mara.
p. cm. — (Sports on the edge!)
Includes bibliographical references and index.
Summary: "Explores the sport of extreme BMX"-Provided by publisher
ISBN 978-1-60870-227-5 (print) ISBN 978-1-60870-747-8 (ebook)
1. Bicycle motocross—Juvenile literature. 2. Extreme sports—Juvenile literature. I. Title.
GV1049.3.M35 2012
796.6'2-dc22
2010013834

EDITOR: Christine Florie PUBLISHER: Michelle Bisson
ART DIRECTOR: Anahid Hamparian SERIES DESIGNER: Kristen Branch

EXPERT READER: Dan Mooney, ABA/BMXer Magazine

Photo research by Marybeth Kavanagh

Cover photo by AP Photo/Lori Shepler
The photographs in this book are used by permission and through the courtesy of: *AP Photo*: Pat Little, 4; Ivan Sekretarev, 29; *Everett Collection*: 6; Mirrorpix, 9, 25; *Alamy*: Buzz Pictures, 12; Steven May, 17; *Getty Images*: Christian Pondella, 10; Harry How, 16; Schwinn, 20; Jonathan Daniel, 22 (bottom), 33; Jeff Gross, 36; Ben Liebenberg/WireImage, 38; *Aurora Photos*: Lisa Seaman, 15; Kirk Mastin, 27; *Dan Mooney*/ABA: 18, 41; *The Image Works*: Topham, 22 (top); Jeff Greenberg, 31; *Linda Elliott*: 35

Printed in Malaysia (T)
1 3 5 6 4 2

CONTENTS

ONE

BMX HISTORY 101

BMX, ALSO KNOWN AS bicycle **motocross**, is one of the most exciting sports in the world. You use a bicycle in one of two ways—to race against others or to perform mind-blowing stunts and tricks. This second form of BMX is known as **freestyle**. One of the best things about BMX is that just about anyone can do it—all you need is the right kind of bike, some safety equipment, and a place to ride.

← BMX, SHORT FOR BICYCLE MOTOCROSS, IS AN EXTREME SPORT FOR ANYONE WHO KNOWS HOW TO RIDE A BIKE AND IS A BIT OF A DAREDEVIL. THE SPORT HAS TWO FORMS: ONE IS RACING (LEFT), THE OTHER IS FREESTYLE (PERFORMING AMAZING STUNTS).

ON ANY SUNDAY

A Cinema 5 Release
From Bruce Brown who made 'Endless Summer'
Rated G

THE MOVIE *ON ANY SUNDAY*
WAS THE INSPIRATION BEHIND
BMX AND ITS SOON-TO-BE
CULT FOLLOWING IN THE
UNITED STATES.

How Did It Start?

BMX began in the United States in the early 1960s. Back then, kids were riding their bikes around dirt tracks to imitate their motorcycle heroes. It was also around this time that the letters *BMX* were first used. Motorcycle racing was often called MX—short for motocross—and the letter *B* was added for *bicycle*.

For a long time BMX was popular in only one part of the United States—southern California. That changed in July 1971, when movie theaters began showing a motorcycle documentary called *On Any Sunday*. In the opening scene, a group of kids are shown zooming around on BMX bikes, pretending to be motorcycle guys. This captured the imagination of soon-to-be BMX fans across the country, and the film became a cult hit.

GETTING BIGGER, GETTING BETTER

BMX saw huge growth in the 1970s. In 1974 the **National Bicycle League** was formed, followed by the **American Bicycle Association** in 1977. Both made BMX better by organizing hundreds of races. In 1976 the first big BMX magazine, *Bicycle Motocross Action*, was published. It had full-color photos and great articles, and thousands of BMX riders also became BMX readers. Racing was the most popular activity at the end of the decade, but performing tricks was catching up fast.

In 1981 BMX got another boost when it was featured in the megahit film *E. T.: The Extra-Terrestrial*. By then there were BMX tracks from New York to California and all points in between. Another hot BMX movie was *RAD*, released in 1986, about a local kid who aspires to race with the pros. It also features amazing freestyle action, and by the late 1980s tricks

THE ABA AND THE NBL

THE TWO LARGEST BMX organizations are the American Bicycle Association (ABA) and the National Bicycle League (NBL). Both manage dozens of events each year, not just in the United States but also in Canada and Mexico. They give out awards to top riders, keep a point system based on a rider's finishes during a year, and have a hall of fame. Both have excellent websites that allow you to find tracks and races in your area, follow the point system and team standings, and keep up on the latest BMX news.

The ABA alone has more than two hundred tracks nationwide, and most offer bicycle and gear rentals, as well as the opportunity to practice during evening and night hours. It also offers riding clinics for kids just starting out.

and stunts were becoming as popular as races. It wasn't long before freestyle had a following all its own.

TV Time

By the end of the 1980s, interest in BMX started to cool down. Many of the kids who had started the BMX boom weren't kids anymore.

BY THE 1980S FREESTYLE RIDING WAS PICKING UP SPEED AS KIDS ACROSS THE UNITED STATES TRIED OUT NEW HEART-STOPPING STUNTS.

The Many Styles of Freestyle

BY THE TIME FREESTYLE became huge, there were several different types of stunts being performed. They are still popular today.

Flatland is a freestyle form in which the rider stays on a flat surface and performs tricks with only himself and the bike. Park is a type of freestyle in which the rider performs tricks with the aid of the equipment found in a skate park. Trail is a style in which the rider performs stunts with the help of dirt-packed jumps. Street involves riding or sliding along obstacles that aren't meant for bicycles, like stairways and handrails. And vert, probably the most dangerous freestyle form, uses a half-pipe—a U-shaped ramp similar in design to a swimming pool, but with curves on the inside ends instead of corners (left). As the 1990s came to an end, BMX products were hot again, and this time the audience was a whole new generation of kids.

A BMX'ER COMPETES AT THE FIRST X GAMES IN RHODE ISLAND IN 1995.

They had cars, jobs, and families. In 1995 new life was injected into the sport when the cable channel ESPN (Entertainment Sports Programming Network) featured some of the more wild freestyle stunts in the first **X Games** broadcast.

Another BMX frenzy erupted in the 2000s when, in 2003, the International Olympic Committee agreed to feature BMX events in the 2008 Summer Olympic Games. Races were held on an oval dirt track and watched live by more than 20,000 fans.

GETTING STARTED

TWO

WHERE'S THE BEST place to ride? Which bike should I get? What kind of safety gear should I wear? All these questions—and plenty more—need to be answered before you begin your quest for BMX greatness.

WHERE TO GO

The best place to ride depends a lot on what kind of BMX you want to do. If racing is your thing, you should go online and see if there are any official tracks in your area. If there are, you probably won't be allowed to ride on them just to practice. (Track owners want to keep them in good condition for race days.) But at least you'll know where to go when you're ready for some real racing. In the meantime, you can sharpen your skills on a practice track. This can be anything from a path in the woods to a series of cones, boxes, or chalk lines in a parking lot.

If freestyle is more your thing, remember that different types of freestyle require different environments. For example, if you want to become a flatlander, all you really need is a smooth surface.

A SKATE PARK IS THE BEST PLACE TO BE TO TRY OUT THE PARK FORM OF BMX FREESTYLE.

IN STREET FREESTYLE, RIDERS USE OBJECTS SUCH
AS STAIRS AND RAILS TO PERFORM TRICKS ON.

Again, a parking lot is as good a place as any. A big driveway also works. Park, on the other hand, involves doing tricks using the contours of a skate park. And street can be done just where the name suggests—on the many objects you'll find in and around an ordinary street.

Some Basic Riding Tips

Keep in mind a few safety tips that'll make your life easier. First, don't ride alone. Accidents are going to happen no matter how good you get, and you don't want to be by yourself when they do. At the very least, bring a cell phone along in case of emergencies. Second, don't ride where there are moving cars or other obvious dangers. Third, avoid riding on private property; there are plenty of public places where biking is allowed.

Also, don't forget to keep your shoelaces tied tight and your pant leg wrapped in rubber bands—you don't want either getting snagged by the bike's

NEVER VENTURE OUT TO THE PARK OR TRACK WITHOUT A HELMET.

chain. Finally, wear your safety equipment. At the very least, *always* wear a helmet. Remember—there's really no such thing as a minor head injury.

THIS RIDER WEARS THE TYPICAL BMX'ER SAFETY GEAR.

SAFETY GEAR

Pretty much every part of your body should be covered when you ride. Pads and helmets can be replaced easily after a crash. Teeth and bones . . . not so much.

Long pants and long-sleeved shirts are better than shorts and T-shirts. Clothing designed for BMXers is made of a tough material that can handle abuse without ripping or tearing. The fabric also has tiny holes for letting air through, keeping you cool.

Pads and guards are cushions that attach to your body either by straps, buttons, Velcro, or by simply being pulled on. They cover your knees, shins, elbows, and wrists.

Some helmets do not cover for your face, whereas others have a part that curves around your mouth.

You can buy goggles separately. Make sure your helmet fits right. Too loose, and it will wobble around and slide down in front of your eyes. Too tight, and it won't fit over your head properly. Gloves are available that have a tough outer coating to protect your hands from scrapes and bruises.

Finally, your bike should also have some padding on it. There are durable foam-rubber pads available to cover the frame's top tube, the crossbar of the handlebars, and the neck.

Your Bike

There are bikes designed specifically for racing and others specifically for freestyle. No matter what you end up getting, remember that you don't have to spend a lot of money on your first bike. Your first bike will most likely get pretty banged up, so save the big money for when all of your amateur "oops" moments are in the past.

There are several differences between a racing bike and a freestyle bike. A racing bike usually has a frame

The Bike That Started It All— The Sting-Ray

IN THE EARLY DAYS there were no bicycles made specifically for BMX. Bikes were just another way of getting around. Then the Schwinn company—one of the biggest bicycle manufacturers in the world—got wise and introduced a new model in 1963 called the Sting-Ray. It was the first bike with BMX in mind. It was low to the ground and had a long seat, high handlebars, and precision steering for making quick turns. While it might look kind of goofy compared to today's rides, it was the biggest thing going back then. Schwinn sold millions of them.

made of aluminum, which is very light. A racing bike also has a large **sprocket** on the front wheel and a small one on the back wheel. A racing bike's rims have **spokes** and, like the frame, are made of aluminum. The best racing tires have rows of little knobs on their treads, which give them good **traction**, and are called **knobbies**. A racing bike often has only one brake, for the back wheel.

A freestyle bike is heavier and tougher. The frame is made from **chromoly**, a type of steel that can handle abuse better than aluminum. The front sprocket is often only a little bigger than the back one. A freestyle bike may also have **mag wheels**. These are made from durable plastic or graphite and have large "arms" connecting the hub to the rim. Freestyle tires are smoother and wider than knobbies, providing better balance for the rider. A freestyle bike will have brakes for both the front and back wheels, and the brake cables will run through a **rotor** (or detangler) so the rider can spin the handlebars without the cables getting caught. Freestyle bikes also have **pegs**

RACING BIKES (ABOVE) AND FREESTYLE BIKES (RIGHT) ARE NOT THE SAME. RACING BIKES HAVE LIGHTER FRAMES, WHICH ARE BETTER FOR SPEED. FREESTYLE FRAMES, ON THE OTHER HAND, ARE HEAVIER AND TOUGHER BECAUSE FREESTYLE RIDING CAN BE VERY ROUGH.

for riders to stand on while performing certain stunts. Pegs are vital to the street form of freestyle, as they are often the part of the bike that will slide or grind on hard surfaces.

Good Old Common Sense

The information here is designed to help you get started with your BMX adventures. If you use a little common sense when purchasing your first bike, ride only in the places you're supposed to ride, and always wear the safety gear designed to keep your injuries to a minimum, you can look forward to years of fun.

TRICKS AND STUNTS YOU CAN DO

EVEN A BEGINNER CAN get into simple freestyle and racing activities. The key to becoming good is to practice often. And remember again that safety should be your greatest concern.

FREESTYLE

The **bunny hop** is probably the most basic of all freestyle moves. Put simply, a bunny hop is lifting the entire bike off the ground using nothing but your body. Here is how to do it.

1. Make sure you have a smooth, flat surface and plenty of room.

2. While riding slowly, stand up on the pedals. Then crouch your body into a squatting position while leaning forward.

3. Pull up on the handlebars so the front wheel comes off the ground.

4. Once the front wheel is in the air, tuck your legs together and pull your knees up. This should pull the back wheel off the ground as well.

5. After the bike is fully airborne, lean forward a little more to make the wheels level.

6. Learn to relax your body upon landing. If you are too stiff, the shock of the landing will be absorbed by your knees and elbows—ouch!

Another basic stunt is the **wheelie**. This is where you pull the front wheel off the ground and ride on only the back one.

POPPING THE FRONT END OF A BIKE INTO THE AIR IS CALLED A WHEELIE.

1. Find a smooth surface and some open space.
2. Riding along at a modest speed, lean back to shift your weight toward the rear of the bike.
3. Pull up on the handlebars to get the front wheel off the ground. At the same time, lean forward slightly so your weight keeps the bike balanced in its new position. On the first few tries, one of two things may happen: the front of the bike will quickly fall down again, or you will fall backward off the bike. Getting the front wheel to just the right height will take some practice.
4. Once you are comfortable with Step 3, learn to keep pedaling with your feet. Soon you will be able to ride along with the front wheel in the air.

Then there's the **endo**. The word is short for "end over end." An endo is like a reverse wheelie—the back wheel comes off the ground instead of the front.

1. Riding along slowly, squeeze the lever of your front brakes only. At the same time,

AN ENDO IS A REVERSE WHEELIE; THE BACK END OF THE BIKE POPS UP.

push the handlebars forward, but shift your weight back slightly to stay balanced. The back wheel should come off the ground.

2. As the rear wheel rises and the seat comes up beneath you, fold yourself into a crouched position.

3. As the rear wheel goes back down, shift your weight forward again.

This trick can also be done on a sidewalk curb, where the endo begins as soon as the front wheel touches the curb. You should still use your front brake, however, to keep the wheel from rolling.

Racing

Most BMX races only last about a minute, so you need to get moving fast. You will line up with your opponents at a starting gate—a long strip of wood that blocks you from getting onto the track. Stand up on both pedals and, when the gate drops, push forward with all your strength. Getting a good start can make all the difference.

Turns in a BMX race are called **berms** and are raised on one side. With a berm, tilting your bike to one side in order to ride the turn is not necessary, since you are already tilted. Turns are a good place to pass opponents, particularly on the inside, because the inside route is shorter in length than the outside route.

Most BMX tracks have obstacles known as **jumps**, and they come in all shapes and sizes. Some have rounded tops; others have flat tops. A few appear as ripples, and a couple look like ramps. They also have

RIDERS TAKE A CURVE, OR BERM, IN THIS BMX RACE.

names that range from sensible to silly, including table-tops, step-ups, step-downs, doubles, triples, rollers, kickers, and whoop-de-doos.

There are two basic ways to take a jump during a race: get enough air to fly over it or actually ride over it. If you try the first one, make sure you can go the distance. If you ride over it instead, keep a firm grip on the handlebars, but relax your body and let the bike move over it naturally.

Finally, straight sections of a BMX track are called straightaways. A straightaway is a good place to pedal hard and build up speed. Remember, though, that

A Wild Ride—Downhill Racing

JUST AS ITS NAME suggests, downhill BMX racing involves a track that runs down a hill. Most downhill tracks go one way rather than in a loop—you start at the top of the hill and end at the bottom. While downhill racing is very exciting, it is also more dangerous than normal racing. You go much faster, brake harder, and get more scratches and bruises if you crash.

THESE THREE BMX'ERS CATCH AIR AS THEY TAKE
A JUMP DURING A RACE.

most straightaways end at some point, either at a
bump or a turn. Always be prepared for these changes.
For example, slow down a little when you come to a
sweeper turn—too fast, and the bike will slide out
from under you.

FOUR

HALL OF FAMERS

BMX HAS ITS SHARE of heroes—guys who have captured the public's attention through their super skills and amazing achievements. These are the ones who were willing to take the biggest risks and earned the greatest rewards. They have not only electrified the BMX world but also defined it.

AN OLD-SCHOOL LEGEND

"Stompin' Stu" Thomsen was BMX's first superstar. He was born in 1958 in southern California and began racing at the age of fifteen. A year later he had already won his first national race. He was known for his blazing speed and his fierce desire to win. He scored lots of big-money victories throughout the rest of the 1970s and well into the 1980s. He also helped design several bikes and tracks. A serious shoulder injury in 1985 forced him to race less, but even today he can be found out there in the dust and dirt once in a while.

When Stompin' Stu won his first national race in 1974, Dave Mirra was just getting around to being born. However, he seemed determined to catch up with Stu pretty quickly. He began riding BMX when he was just four years old. He started as a flatlander but soon

DAVE MIRRA TAKES FIRST PLACE AFTER THE BMX PARK FINAL OF THE NIKE 6.0 BMX OPEN IN JUNE 2009. (GARRETT REYNOLDS TOOK SECOND AND MARCUS TOOKER TOOK THIRD.)

moved into park and vert. He had two sponsorships by the time he was thirteen and was performing in major competitions. By the early 1990s he was regularly earning first- and second-place finishes. In 1994 he was forced to stop riding for over a year after being hit by a car. After his recovery, he became a regular at the X Games, where he earned more medals than anyone.

Also in Mirra's class was Mat Hoffman, who became another freestyle legend. When Hoffman began entering contests—at the age of thirteen—his thing was vert. His most valuable talent, it seemed, was a lack of fear—he would try stunts others wouldn't dare. He broke a world record for greatest height reached from riding off a ramp—over 50 feet off the ground. He also invented more than a hundred new tricks. The bikes he rode took an enormous beating. After most of them fell apart, he began designing his own. That led him to start a company called Hoffman Bikes. He has also been involved in the production of television programs and video games.

GIRLS CAN DO IT, TOO!

BORN IN CALIFORNIA in 1970, Cheri Elliott started racing seriously before the age of ten. She won the first competition she ever entered and quickly established herself as the best female racer in the country. By 1983 she had won several national championships, and two years later she was considered the top female racer in the world. She retired from BMX in 1986, then got involved with mountain-bike racing in 1994. Showing the same amazing talent, she went on to win more than a dozen major titles. She was elected to the U.S. Bicycling Hall of Fame in 2008.

Across the Pond

On the other side of the Atlantic Ocean was Jamie Bestwick. Born in England in 1971, he never thought he would become a BMX sensation on par with Mirra and Hoffman. By the time he was ten, he was still just riding around with his friends, doing a little racing and freestyle. His favorite was vert. He came to the United States to compete in the X Games in 1996, where he earned a third-place finish. In the 2000 Games, he accomplished what many thought impossible—he beat Dave Mirra and won a gold medal. Throughout the first half of the 2000s, he continued earning top spots in dozens of competitions. He suffered a serious injury in 2006 but returned to BMX soon thereafter and continues competing to this day.

JAMIE BESTWICK WAVES TO FANS AFTER COMPETING IN THE MEN'S BMX FREESTYLE VERT FINAL DURING THE ESPN X GAMES IN CALIFORNIA IN 2006.

FIVE

BMX AROUND THE WORLD

THERE WAS A TIME when BMX was nothing more than a bunch of kids riding around homemade tracks in southern California—but that was during the 1960s, and this is today. Since BMX has become a worldwide rage, there are hundreds of events held every year, and all sorts of organizations that run them. Some of the biggest are listed here, but there may be others much closer to where you live.

THE X GAMES

The heart-stopping X Games are held twice a year by ESPN—winter games in January (sometimes February) and summer games in August. The X stands for "extreme." These sports involve high levels of danger from extreme height, speed, and the potential loss of control. Common events include bungee jumping, sky surfing, mountain boarding, street luge, cliff diving, wakeboarding and, of course, various forms of BMX. Winners of each competition are awarded medals similar to those of the Olympic Games—gold, silver, and bronze—as well as prize money.

GRAND NATIONALS

Two of the biggest BMX race events in the United States are the grand nationals. Each of the leading BMX organizations—the ABA and the NBL—holds a grand national every year. The NBL has theirs in September, the ABA in November. There are dozens of races for various age and gender classes. The top pros come to win prizes, money, and a chance to claim the title as the best racer in the world. The overall winner gets to wear the coveted "No. 1" plate on his bike for a year. Amateurs are welcome, too—they race in their own

ESPN'S X GAMES ARE A THRILL TO WATCH.
BMX'ERS FROM ALL OVER THE WORLD FLIRT WITH
DANGER AS THEY PUSH THE LIMITS OF HEIGHT,
SPEED, AND SANITY.

THE MAN BEHIND THE NBL

GEORGE ESSER had a huge effect on BMX without entering a single race or performing any freestyle stunts. In 1974 he formed the National Bicycle League after deciding he didn't like the way the National Bicycle Association—the biggest BMX organization at the time—was managing the racetracks his two sons used. Esser thought BMX should be more about the kids and less about making a profit. He designed the NBL to be a true democracy—everyone involved was allowed to speak his mind. Soon it was the most powerful BMX organization in the eastern half of the United States (while the NBA disappeared in 1981). Esser died in 2006, but his NBL is still going strong.

class, attend clinics given by the pros, and show off their skills to potential sponsors. It is also a chance to meet other riders from around the country.

MISSION POSSIBLE: HAVE FUN

It's always good to know what bike is best for the kind of riding you do, why it's better to pass someone on

BMX IS AN EXTREME SPORT WHERE ALL RIDERS CAN ENJOY THE THRILL OF EXECUTING AMAZING STUNTS OR GETTING TO THE FINISH LINE FIRST.

the inside of a turn rather than the outside, or how to pull a wheelie without falling off your bike. But first and foremost, BMX is supposed to be *fun*. It's a profession for some, and a lucky few have become rich and famous from it. But even those dudes are still enjoying themselves.

BMX is one of the most thrilling sports in the world, and any kid with a bike can do it. So call up your friends, get out there, and have a good time.

And don't hurt yourself!

GLOSSARY

American Bicycle Association one of the first major BMX sanctioning organizations, formed in 1977

berm a turn on a BMX racetrack that is raised on one side

bunny hop the act of lifting a bike completely off the ground while riding

chromoly a tough metal alloy used to make BMX frames, usually for freestyle

endo the act of raising the rear wheel off the ground, then bringing it down again

freestyle the type of BMX that focuses on tricks and stunts rather than racing

jump a raised area on a BMX track with a rounded top

knobbies tires with many small knobs sticking out of the treads

mag wheels wheels with only a few large and sturdy rods that connect the hub to the rim

motocross sport of racing bicycles or motorcycles

National Bicycle League the first major BMX sanctioning organization, formed in 1974

pegs short metal rods that stick out from the center of a bicycle's wheels

rotor a device attached to the handlebars of a bicycle that allows them to be spun around without tangling the brake cables

spoke narrow metal rod that attaches a wheel's hub to its rim

sprocket toothed wheel that guides a bicycle's chain as the rider pushes forward on the pedals

traction a tire's ability to grip the surface upon which it is riding

sweeper turn a turn on a track that is flat to the ground

wheelie the act of raising the front wheel off the ground, holding it in the air, and then bringing it down again

X Games annual sporting event involving a variety of extreme-action games, such as skateboarding, skiing, snowboarding, and BMX

FIND OUT MORE

BOOKS

Hon, Shek. *BMX Riding Skills: The Guide to Flatland Tricks*. Westport, CT: Firefly Books, 2010.

McClellan, Ray. *BMX Freestyle*. Minneapolis, MN: Bellwether Media, 2008.

——. *Downhill BMX*. Minneapolis, MN: Bellwether Media, 2008.

Peterson Kaelberer, Angie. *BMX Racing*. Mankato, MN: Capstone Press, 2006.

Savage, Jeff. *Dave Mirra*. Minneapolis, MN: Lerner Publications, 2007.

Woods, Bob. *Mat Hoffman*. Minneapolis, MN: Child's World, 2006.

WEBSITES

ABA BMX

www.ababmx.com/

Home page for the American Bicycle Association. News, race schedules, loads of color photos, factory and sponsorship information, and plenty more.

BMX Freestyler

www.bmxfreestyler.com

> Up-to-the-minute news and other information
> about all forms of freestyle. Also includes many
> videos of both amateurs and pros performing
> their latest stunts.

NBL BMX

www.nbl.org

> The National Bicycle League—the longest-running
> BMX organization in America. Information on
> the latest races, news, and NBL programs. A good
> starting point for BMX beginners.

Vital BMX

www.vitalbmx.com

> An enthusiastically run site with news, product
> reviews, photos and videos, and more.

INDEX

Page numbers in **boldface** are illustrations.

ABOUT THE AUTHOR

A BMX enthusiast since childhood, **WIL MARA** is also the award-winning author of more than 120 books. He has written both fiction and nonfiction for children and adults. You can find more information about his work at www.wilmara.com.